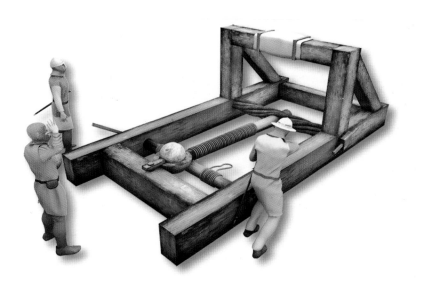

Published in 2013 by The Rosen Publishing Group, Inc.
29 East 21st Street, New York, NY 10010

Copyright © 2013 Weldon Owen Pty Ltd. Originally published in 2011 by Discovery Communications, LLC

Original copyright © 2011 Discovery Communications, LLC. Discovery Education™ and the Discovery Education logo are trademarks of Discovery Communications, LLC, used under license. All rights reserved.

Photo Credits: **KEY** tl=top left; tc=top center; tr=top right; cl=center left; c=center; cr=center right; bl=bottom left; bc=bottom center; br=bottom right; bg=background
iS = istockphoto.com; KC = Kobal: PIC = The Picture Desk: TF = Topfoto
6c iS; **6–7**cr iS; **7**br, c, cl, tc iS; **8**tl PIC; **10**tl iS; tc TF; **10–11**bg iS; **11**br iS; **13**tr iS; **14–15**bg iS; **15**br iS; **17**tr iS; **18**br, cl, cr iS; **18–19**bg iS; **19**br, tr iS; **20**cl iS; **20–21**bg iS; **21**bc iS; **23**bc, br iS; **25**br iS; br TF; **27**tc iS; **28**br, tr iS; br, tr TF; **29**bl, br, tl, tr iS; bl, br, tl, tr iS

All illustrations copyright Weldon Owen Pty Ltd

Weldon Owen Pty Ltd
Managing Director: Kay Scarlett
Creative Director: Sue Burk
Publisher: Helen Bateman
Senior Vice President, International Sales: Stuart Laurence
Vice President Sales North America: Ellen Towell
Administration Manager, International Sales: Kristine Ravn

Library of Congress Cataloging-in-Publication Data

Park, Louise, 1961–
 Life in the Middle Ages / by Louise Park.
    p. cm. — (Discovery education: ancient civilizations)
 Includes index.
 ISBN 978-1-4777-0055-6 (library binding) — ISBN 978-1-4777-0095-2 (pbk.) —
ISBN 978-1-4777-0096-9 (6-pack)
1. Middle Ages—Juvenile literature. 2. Europe—History—476-1492—Juvenile literature. 3. Europe—Social life and customs—Juvenile literature. 4. Civilization, Medieval—Juvenile literature. I. Title.
 CB351.P323 2013
 940.1—dc23

                                    2012019578

Manufactured in the United States of America

CPSIA Compliance Information: Batch #W12PK2: For Further Information contact Rosen Publishing, New York, New York at 1-800-237-9932

ANCIENT CIVILIZATIONS

LIFE IN THE MIDDLE AGES

LOUISE PARK

PowerKiDS
press.

New York

Contents

Medieval Societ

The medieval period took place in Europe from around 1000 to the 1500s. This period was known as the Middle Ages and its society had a very defined structure. Medieval society lived by a strict social arrangement called the feudal system. This system was shaped like a pyramid: the king was at the top; the barons and knights below him; and the farmers and serfs were at the bottom. Everyone within the system was linked by a set of rights and responsibilities.

The king
The king held all the power, owned all the land, and governed the people. He granted the barons some of his land, which they could pass on to their heirs. In return, the barons were loyal to the king and provided men to fight for him in times of war.

Barons, bishops, and crusaders
Barons were noblemen who gave knights land in exchange for loyalty. Bishops had similar status to barons and a lot of worldly power. The crusaders were knights who fought in the name of God.

Knights
Knights were men from high-ranking families who were well-trained in horsemanship and warfare. They swore to be loyal to their lord, served him in battle, and were granted land in exchange.

Farmers, laborers, and serfs
These people made up about 90 percent of the social pyramid. They lived and worked on land owned by barons or knights. They worked to pay their rent. Most were tied to the land and their owners.

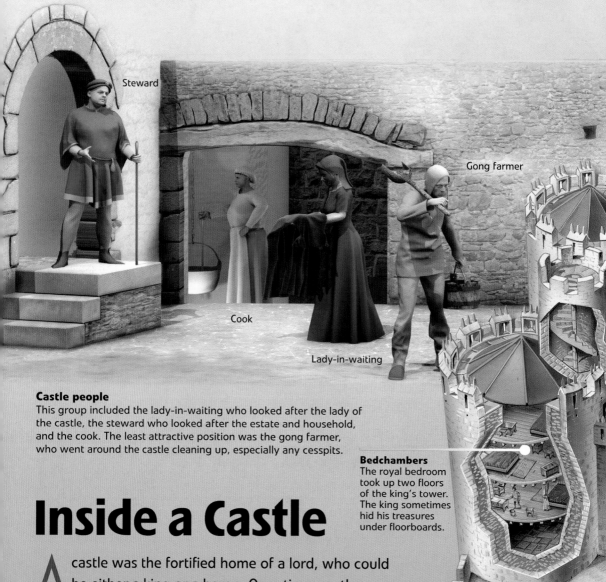

Steward

Gong farmer

Cook

Lady-in-waiting

Castle people
This group included the lady-in-waiting who looked after the lady of the castle, the steward who looked after the estate and household, and the cook. The least attractive position was the gong farmer, who went around the castle cleaning up, especially any cesspits.

Bedchambers
The royal bedroom took up two floors of the king's tower. The king sometimes hid his treasures under floorboards.

Inside a Castle

A castle was the fortified home of a lord, who could be either a king or a baron. Over time, castles became more and more sophisticated. There were generally two wards inside the castle wall. The outer ward housed the stables and workshops, and the inner ward was the main part of the castle that housed the kitchens, chapel, Great Hall, and the bedchambers of the noble family who lived there.

Trapdoor
idden door in the Great
allowed prisoners to be
en to the dungeons in a
speedy manner.

Great Hall
Prisoners were brought
before the king in the
Great Hall. Banquets
were also held here.

Arrow loops

Drawbridge

Repairs
A large wheel and
pulley system
lifted heavy rocks
and stones
needed to repair
to the castle.

Building a castle

The first castles were built from
wood, but rebuilt in stone to make
them stronger and more difficult to
attack. People dug ditches around
castles, filled them with water, and
turned them into moats. Eventually,
castles became enormous structures
with 16-foot- (5 m) thick walls and
huge towers filled with archers.

Hunting

The upper class hunted to provide food as well as for sport. They often used dogs to hunt deer and boars while they followed on horseback. They also trained falcons, hawks, kestrels, and other birds of prey to attack pigeons and pheasants.

Banquet for the lord

Great feasts were very much a part of the noble family tradition. The lord sat at the highest table farthest from the kitchen. His household and guests sat on benches that stretched down the hall, with the poorest being farthest from the high table.

Elaborate dishes

Banquets sometimes featured exotic animals, such as peacock. The skin was stripped off before cooking, then sewn back on, along with the plumage.

Leisure and Entertainment

Although there was always much work to be done at the castle, there was also opportunity for leisure activities. No work was ever done on a Sunday as it was seen as a day of rest. Listening to music, playing chess, hunting, and even playing ball games were among the more popular leisure pastimes.

Musicians
Standing in the gallery above the Great Hall, musicians played trumpets, lutes, harps, and other medieval instruments.

Jester
Providing light entertainment, the jester told jokes, sang songs, delivered riddles, and danced.

MAKING MUSIC

Woodwind and brass instruments were played at most of the ceremonies that took place in the Great Hall. At intimate ceremonies, musicians would play love songs on the lute or flutes.

Trumpet

Lute

Recorder

Shawm

Rebec

Farming the Land

Most people who lived during the Middle Ages worked on the land. Peasants worked and lived on the estates of noblemen and knights. They farmed the land all through the changing seasons to maximize harvest and productivity.

A plowed field ready for sowing

A field of growing wheat

Winter
Wood was cut and fences were built. Workers spread manure on fields to fertilize the soil. Tools were also built and repaired in winter.

Seeds lay dormant ready to grow in spring.

Fallow field was used as a sports field.

New fallow field

...ring
...rkers plowed the fields
... sowed seeds into the
...und. These would grow
... be harvested in the fall.
...ey also took care of newborn
...stock, such as baby lambs.

Summer
Wheat was harvested.
The sheep were shorn for
their wool and the grass
was cut for cattle feed.

...ll
...ts and barley were
...rvested, pigs were let
...se to fatten on acorns,
...ney and apples were
...rvested, and grapes were
...essed to make wine.

TAXING WORKERS
A peasant or serf had to give
away 60 percent of his crop.
This left little for his family.

10% to church

25% to lord

25% for seed to
plant next year

40% for
peasant
and family

Shorn wool
goes to the
market.

The wheat
harvest

Fallow field

Field was plowed and sown for
next summer's wheat harvest.

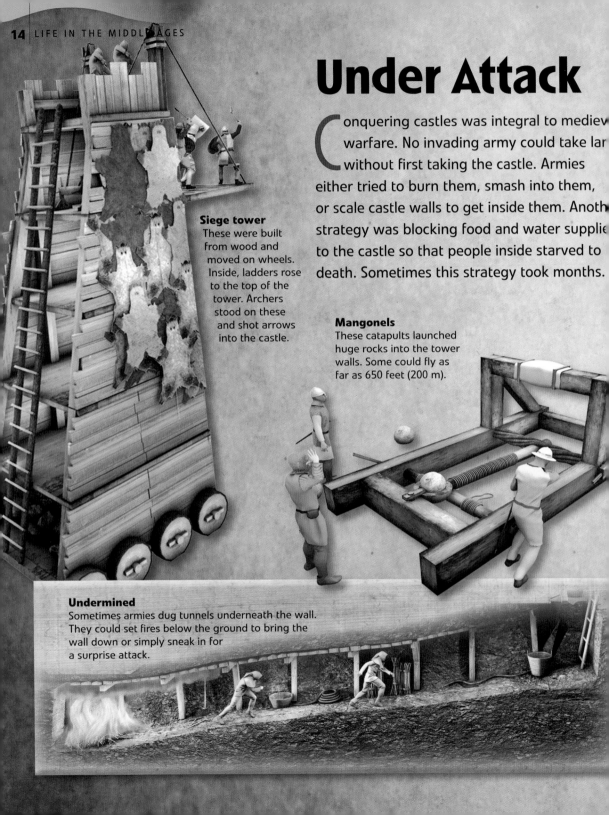

Under Attack

Conquering castles was integral to mediev warfare. No invading army could take lar without first taking the castle. Armies either tried to burn them, smash into them, or scale castle walls to get inside them. Anoth strategy was blocking food and water supplie to the castle so that people inside starved to death. Sometimes this strategy took months.

Siege tower
These were built from wood and moved on wheels. Inside, ladders rose to the top of the tower. Archers stood on these and shot arrows into the castle.

Mangonels
These catapults launched huge rocks into the tower walls. Some could fly as far as 650 feet (200 m).

Undermined
Sometimes armies dug tunnels underneath the wall. They could set fires below the ground to bring the wall down or simply sneak in for a surprise attack.

Storming the gatehouse

A strategic attack generally focused on the gatehouse or one of the towers along the castle walls.

Deadly rain
Boiling water and hot oil were poured onto people below though holes called machicolations.

Push off!
Ladders were used to climb into the castle, but most climbers fell to their deaths as castle defenders pushed the ladder over with a long pole.

Portcullis
A heavy gate made from wood and iron was the last line of defense.

SIEGE MISSILES

Stones were the most effective projectiles, but armies also used flaming pots, hot liquids, and even dead, diseased animals.

Boiled liquids

Round stones

Firepots

Boulders

Dead animals

Into Battle

Knights trained and fought very differently than the armies of today. They trained separately in their own household group, and battle tactics were simple yet effective. Knights charged their opponents on horseback, which gave them an advantage over men fighting on foot. However, the horses could be hard to turn once knights were engaged in a battle. The biggest army was not always the winner, and battles were more often won based on clever battle tactics.

Decoy can
Armies pitched dec
tents as a target for t
opposing arm

Bait
A smaller group of knights protected by spearmen pretended to be the main army.

A battle begins

The element of surprise, and holding back the charge, was one of the most successful battle tactics of medieval times. In this battle, the blue army charges the red and looks set to win. However, most of the red army is hidden away, waiting for the right moment to attack and conquer.

KNIGHTS' LAST STAND

If a knight was thrown from his horse, he was very vulnerable. Once down, he was attacked by skilled pikemen or swordmen, and was also exposed to archers.

A knight suffers a deadly blow.

Archers
A team of archers was strategically placed and held back safely. When the time was right, they unleashed a wave of arrows into the rushing army to confuse them.

Knights' charge
The knights' charge often had an enormous impact in battle and was used to smash the front of the opposing army.

Surprise attackers
Once the blues are committed to the charge, the hidden red army strikes from the flank and is likely to defeat the army.

Becoming a Knigh

At the age of seven, a boy who was to become a knight was sent away, usually to the house of a relative, to become a page. At the age of 14, he w apprenticed to a knight in his castle as a squire. After th followed five years of training before he could serve as fully trained knight. Due to the cost of armor and horse only boys from the richest families could become knigh

School

A page was taught subjects such as geography, history, religion, and basic reading and writing. He was taught by the castle chaplain.

Table manners

The page would serve the lord at his ta He was taught good manners and wou be beaten if he did not follow them.

Learning to fight

Training was important. Squires fought with wooden swords and shields. They also kept fit with wrestling and other physical training.

Learning to joust
Squires practiced fighting on horseback with a machine called a quintain. After striking the target, they had to avoid being knocked off their horse by a sack on the other end.

Dubbing
A squire was made a knight in a ceremony known as dubbing. He knelt before his lord, who tapped him on the shoulders with his sword and pronounced him a knight.

Armor and Weapo

Knights wore protective armor to increase their chances survival in battle. Early armor was made from leather a mail. This was flexible, but vulnerable to arrows. In the late 1200s, metal plates, known as plate armor, were added. A suit of plate armor weighed up to 55 pounds (25 kg). To defend themselves, knights fought with spears, lances, and swords. They also used weapons such as axes and pikes.

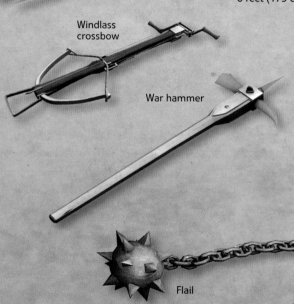

Dagger and sheath

Windlass crossbow

War hammer

Flail

Weapons
Foot soldiers (who wer mainly peasants) used readily available weapo even pitchforks. They a used swords that could measure up to nearly 6 feet (175 cm) long.

HERALDRY

This identification system was used to recognize knights in full armor on the battlefield. A coat of arms was placed on the knight's armor shield, cloth tunic, and sometimes even draped over his horse.

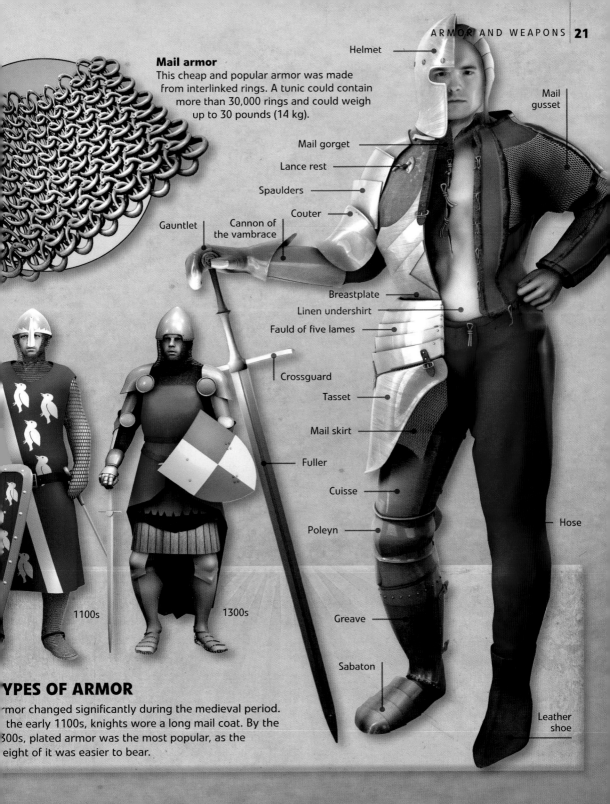

Helmet

Mail gusset

Mail armor
This cheap and popular armor was made from interlinked rings. A tunic could contain more than 30,000 rings and could weigh up to 30 pounds (14 kg).

Mail gorget

Lance rest

Spaulders

Couter

Gauntlet

Cannon of the vambrace

Breastplate

Linen undershirt

Fauld of five lames

Crossguard

Tasset

Mail skirt

Fuller

Cuisse

Poleyn

Hose

Greave

Sabaton

Leather shoe

1100s

1300s

YPES OF ARMOR

rmor changed significantly during the medieval period.
the early 1100s, knights wore a long mail coat. By the
300s, plated armor was the most popular, as the
eight of it was easier to bear.

Practice for War

During peacetime, knights needed to remain fit and keep their skills ready for battle. To do this, knights participated in tournaments of mock battles and other types of combat. From the 1100s, tournaments had become so popular that people began to see them as entertainment. A melee was the mock battle in which many knights, divided into two teams, fought together. Jousts were battles where two men fought each other with lances.

Jousting knights

The aim of the joust was to knock the opponent off his horse. Each knight charged toward their opponent and struck him with their lance. During the 1400s, a barrier called a tilt was used to separate charging knights. Lances were always blunt to prevent any serious injury.

TOURNAMENTS

Tournaments among teams of knights allowed knights to demonstrate and develop their horsemanship and battle skills. The first tournaments were held in the countryside during the 1000s, and the last tournament was staged during the 1600s.

Shaffron

Crinet

Rerebraces

Helme

Going to War

Vambrace and gauntlet

The medieval knight rode into battle covered in full armor that offered protection from swords, arrows, and axes. His horse was also covered in protective armor. If a knight fell off his horse, or his horse was wounded during battle, he was at a great disadvantage.

A knight from the 1500s

Knights from this period wore a full suit of armor for maximum protection and fought with a long sword. Earlier knights wore suits of chain mail and fought with a short sword and shield.

Long sword

Crupper

HORSE ARMOR

A knight's biggest expense was his horse, which also required protection during battle. Horse armor included protection for the head and neck, metal plates that protected the chest and hindquarters, and iron horseshoes. Trappers, or decorative coverings, were also draped over the horse to display the knight's coat of arms.

The armor for a horse's head was called a shaffron.

The End of Castles

An end to castle life began when cannons and gunpowder were introduced. This ammunition provided attackers with a stronger and more practical way to bring down castle walls. Some of the richer nobles could afford to build castles that could withstand cannon fire, but most could not. Also, by the 1400s and 1500s, kings were relying more on armies of mercenaries. This meant they no longer needed military service from barons, so barons did not need castles.

Did You Know?

Castles were cold and uncomfortable dwellings. When they were no longer needed for safety, nobles moved into grand manors that were equipped with all the latest luxuries.

Gunpowder and cannons

Gunpowder was invented in China more than a thousand years ago. Europeans discovered that it could be useful in cannons only toward the end of the medieval period. Gunpowder allowed cannonballs to be fired with extreme force.

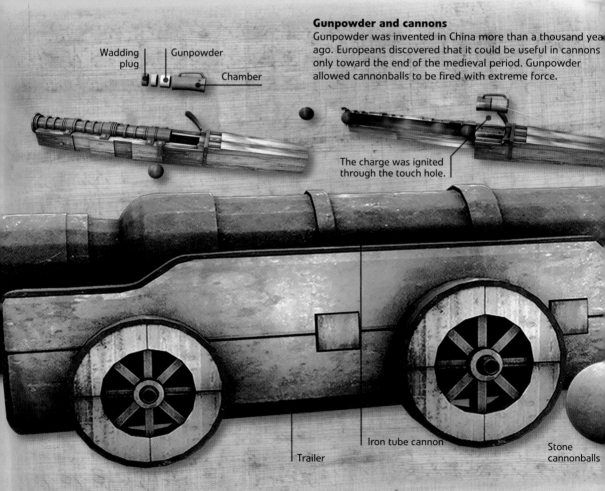

Wadding plug

Gunpowder

Chamber

The charge was ignited through the touch hole.

Trailer

Iron tube cannon

Stone cannonballs

A MIGHTY BLAST

Gunpowder was made from three main ingredients: saltpeter, which came from stale urine and manure; sulfur, which was mined; and charcoal, which was partially burned wood.

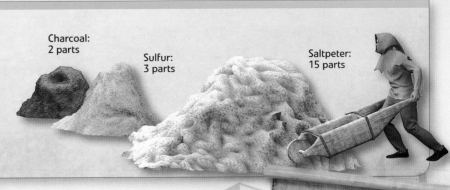

Charcoal:
2 parts

Sulfur:
3 parts

Saltpeter:
15 parts

At the front line

Cannons were most effective when fired at point-blank range. Firing that close to a castle wall meant that gunners were very vulnerable to defender attack. As a result, gunners were paid well to perform their tasks and were highly respected for their bravery. Unfortunately, not many lived to enjoy their salaries.

Famous Warriors

Many knights and warriors were recognized for their bravery and skill in battle and became symbols of heroism throughout history. Over time, the title of knight was granted to people the reigning king or queen felt should be recognized for their achievements. This tradition continues today.

RICHARD THE LIONHEART

King Richard I is remembered as one of England's last great warrior kings. He spent most of his rule fighting the Crusade wars. His bravery and courage earned him the name Lionheart.

CHARLEMAGNE

King Charlemagne established the medieval knights around 774 BC. The knights came from countries that formed part of the king's kingdom, which extended across western Europe to include France, Italy, and Germany.

SIR LANCELOT

Sir Lancelot is remembered in legend as a heroic knight. He was one of King Arthur's Knights of the Round Table of Camelot. He is also remembered for being a romantic and eloping with his love, Queen Guinevere.

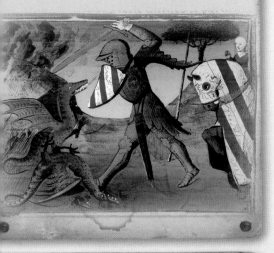

SAINT GEORGE

Saint George is remembered in religious stories for slaying a dragon. It was said that he converted the town of Silene to Christianity after heroically killing the dragon that ravaged their town.

JOAN OF ARC

Joan of Arc is remembered for leading the French army to many important victories during the Hundred Years' War. She claimed she saw visions of God who told her to reclaim French land from the English.

ILYA MUROMETS

Ilya Muromets was a knight from Russia who was thought to have superhuman strength and could fight off invasions single-handedly. Later on, in old age, he became a monk and was canonized by the church.

A Medieval Life

Now it is your turn to be a famous medieval knight!

Imagine that you are a famous medieval knight. Revisit pages 28 and 29 and think about who your favorite knight is and why. Now create your own gallery box that will include your name, a photo, your coat of arms, and information about you and why you are so famous.

Here are some questions to help you with your writing:

1 What knight's name will you give yourself?

2 What will your coat of arms look like?

3 What exceptional skills do you have?

4 What will you be remembered for?

Glossary

sspits (SES-pitz) A pit where uid waste and sewage was posed of.

coy (DEE-koy) A fake mp used to mislead and lure he enemy.

llow (FA-loh) A field that has en plowed, then left unsown a period.

nk (FLANK) The right or left e of the body of an army.

rtification r-tih-fih-KAY-shun) lefensive wall or building t has been erected for ense against attack.

heirs (AYRZ) Persons legally entitled to the property or rank of another upon their death.

mercenaries (MER-suh-ner-eez) Professional soldiers who fought for money.

noblemen (NOH-bul-men) Men who belong to the noble class of a society.

pikemen (PYK-men) Soldiers who are armed and fight with a pike.

serf (SERF) An agricultural laborer bound by the feudal system to work his lord's estate.

warrior (WAR-yur) An experienced and highly successful soldier.

Index

Websites

Due to the changing nature of Internet links, PowerKids Press has developed an online list of websites related to the subject of this book. This site is updated regularly. Please use this link to access the list: www.powerkidslinks.com/disc/mage/